# THE RAT WHO COVERED ITS EYES: 11 Rules For A Post Civil Rights Struggle

DR. RIYAAD GIOVANNI

# DEDICATION

I dedicate this book to the memory of those Black Americans who came before me and gave their lives in search of liberty. I also dedicate this book to my children Javier, Riyaad Jr., Shakurah, Juwaad & Ziporah. May your futures be brighter than I ever could have dreamed. Shout out to the wife for all your support. It's all about the ⊔! **Go Canes**!

# CONTENTS

# FORWARD

The global economy is a place where there is little margin for the slightest error in judgment. You're either the prey or the predator! The hunter or the hunted! It is because of this that I did not want to write a long drawn out book full of egotistical bloviating and impractical advice. This book is concise and straight to the point. I authored this book with the expectation that within 48 hours of receiving it, you will already have begun implementing its tools into practice. I wrote this book with every Black businessperson, sales rep, financier, laymen in mind. Your daily struggle for survival was my sole inspiration for compiling these pages. Some may read this in hopes of being entertained. But what you'll find within the contents of these pages is a strong dose of reality. The subject matter should not be viewed as being negative. It's nothing more than the pure unadulterated truth as I know and understand it.

I'm not in search of fame or recognition for the work I have done. I wrote this strictly out of love for Black people and a profound hatred of oppression. I ask that <u>The Rat That Covered His Eyes: 11 Rules For A Post Civil Rights Struggle</u> be accepted for the very same reason that it was written. I have nothing greater to present than the sum of my life experience and observation, broken down into a mental training regiment.

The economy for Blacks is plagued by mis-education, mis-direction, and lack of leadership. Therefore, it is now that I'm offering my remedy to those hoping to think and move wisely within our global economy. I know some may reject or discard what I have to say, but I remain confident that business will welcome this book with open arms. If one duly pursues the jewels of information contained within and ultimately live them, one will attain those elements of greatness that God and your own merits have predestined.

*"Good people do not need laws to tell them to act responsibly, while bad people will find a way around the laws." - Plato*

## "War Within: The Entrepreneurs Creed"

*Sleep has no use beyond its minimum necessity to maintain life. A thing I once loved, cherished and looked forward to, I now despise. Sleep is a cumbersome monstrosity that somehow has a way of sneaking up at the most inopportune times. Sleep, seduces hunger into a state of forgetfulness. And hunger is much more than a knot in the pit of one's belly. **Desire** is the bastard brother of **determination**. Where **determination** was born in nobility, **desire** was born the bastard child of **lust** and **laziness**. But! **Hunger** is **desires** degenerate general. No warrior was ever so fierce and loyal as **hunger**. Though **hunger** was desperate, reckless and ill-informed. The Entrepreneur who seeks success through integrity is the one for whom **determination** has convinced **desire** to lend **hunger** for battle. The successful entrepreneur empowers and emboldens **determination** while holding **desire** at bay and unleashing **hunger** onto a world in controlled chaos. An entrepreneurs **Desire** must never command **hunger**. And **hunger**, must forever be distracted by the wars of **determination**. If **desire** and **hunger** were to ever rule, integrity would be lost. **Determination** would be murdered. And success would be a mystery, a fairytale… an inaudible whisper. Success can only be a servant of integrity.*

*- Riyaad Giovanni*

9

Dr. Riyaad Giovanni

# Chapter 1 The Rat Who Covered Its Eyes

*"I freed a thousand slaves. I could have freed a thousand
more if only they knew they were slaves." - Harriet
Tubman*

The Rat Who Covered Its Eyes: 11 Rules For A
Post Civil Rights Struggle will begin to demystify
forward progress for Black people in America. But
this book begins with a short story, a fable to be
exact. Before we get into the meat of how to break
our chains of economic dependence on White
society, we must first be in the correct frame of mind
to receive guidance. The following story will allow
you to do just that. Please open your mind and
absorb the wisdom in this story that was handed
down to me by an elder. Unfortunately, I no longer
remember the elder's last name. We simply referred
to him as "Cleveland Ali" as he hailed from
Cleveland, Ohio and there were many by the name

of Ali growing up in Atlanta, Ga. "Cleveland Ali" told us many stories about economic independence and entrepreneurship, but two stories were particularly haunting, "The Rat Who Covered His Eyes" and the other story he so eloquently told was "The Rat Who Grew Too Fat To Find Its Food". But, "The Rat Who Grew To Fat To Find Its Food" is another story for another book.

## THE RAT WHO COVERED HIS EYES

There once was a rat that lived scared in a huddled mass of other rats, inside the walls of a crumbling house. These rats often went hungry. And due to the terrible conditions, rarely got along. One day, out of violent hunger, a rat finally developed the courage to step out of the shadows of the walls and search out in the open for food. As he reluctantly stuck his head out the rat hole, he could see a wheel of cheese lying on the floor. His stomach tightened and he could feel his belly button touching his spine. He slowly crept out of his familiar, scanning the vast openness for the big white cat. This was the same big white cat that ended the life of any rat searching to fill its belly with food out in the open. He inched closer and closer to the wheel of cheese, keeping his head low and submissively scrubbing his belly against the ground. And although his hunger had become unbearable, he simply did not have the courage to boldly go after the food he needed. As the rat slithered even closer to the cheese, he could basically taste it.

Then suddenly the hairs on the back of his neck stood up. He sensed something foreboding. It was at that moment a massive shadow engulfed the rat's entire body, including the cheese. Without warning, the rat-eating cat let out a ferocious hiss that stopped the rat in his tracks. Being scared almost unconscious, all the rat could think to do was be still, cover its eyes, and wait for the inevitable. Quickly, the rat said a prayer. While praying the rat began to hear very loud clanking noises and movement all throughout the room. It was almost as though the cat began chasing its tail around the room or something. But the rat refused to look. With eyes covered, he prayed even harder, praying to disappear. The rat was praying so hard that he didn't even realize all the noise had stopped and the room was filled with silence. After a few minutes of sitting in silence, the rat finally mustered up the strength to uncover his eyes. Slowly he looked up, fully expecting the big white cat to devour him. But it didn't happen. The cat was gone. There...before his very eyes, was the mound of cheese. The rat felt sheer delight! He dove face first into the mound of cheese and ate.

It seemed as though he ate for hours, leaving only a few crumbs behind. In order to prove his astounding journey, the rat took those few crumbs back to the rats inside the walls. As he told his story of how he came across the cheese, most of the other rats didn't believe him. But a few rats, tired of their condition and extremely hungry, hoped he was telling the truth. They believed him enough that they were willing to take a chance with the killer cat. They needed an opportunity to fill their bellies. So the rat decided to let the other rats in on his secret as to how he acquired the cheese. But before taking the journey, some ground rules were laid out. "**Rule one**: must tread slowly. **Rule two**: when the killer cat comes, cover your eyes. And **rule three**: pray when you cover your eyes and you will disappear. The cat will not be able to see you. Once the cat gets tired and leaves, you will be able to eat all the cheese you want. But under no circumstance should you ever look up when you hear the cat. Keep your head down and pray, and your faith in prayer will make you invisible to the big white cat."

The next day the rat and his band of three began the journey of leaving the rat hole. They did everything as they were told. When they saw the shadow of the cat and heard the noise, they immediately covered their eyes and prayed they would disappear. The noises were even louder this time and the cat screeched, hissed and meowed viciously. But just like the day before, the noises subsided. As the rats uncovered their eyes and looked around, they saw two of their friends were missing. The rat surmised they were missing because they lost faith and uncovered their eyes when they should have been praying and keeping their eyes closed.

The three remaining rats ate until their bellies were full. They all took a few crumbs back to the rats inside the walls. The first rat decided that any one who was not willing to take the risk and show

faith initially were not worthy of receiving the
crumbs from the block of cheese. Instead, the lead
rat decided to only take enough cheese back in order
to entice the others. Over time, the first rat
convinced more and more rats to believe in his
methods. He taught them how to pray and cover
their eyes when they were surrounded by danger.
He preached that only those unfaithful few would
be killed by the big white cat. The first rat was so
convincing, that even the other rats that survived
the ordeal began speaking about how those non-
believing rats deserved to die for loosing faith. The
first rat became the de-facto leader over everything
and everyone. He was the political leader, the civic
leader and most importantly, the leader of their
faith.

After making many, many, many trips to the
cheese wheel, the leader had become fat. He became
so comfortable with the process of dealing with the
savage cat, that he no longer feared the cat. As long
as he kept to the rules of praying when trouble came
and keeping his eyes covered, what was there to be
afraid of? Eventually, the many became the few as
the rats had been eaten and dispatched by the cat.
There was only a handful of faithfuls left. On several
trips, all that would be left behind is the first rat and
one of his original friends. Before the last trip they
delighted in their faithfulness. They spoke badly of
the rats that lost their lives. They spoke of how little
faith they had and how disobedient they were.

On a particular day, the two set out for the
day's ration of food, confidently walking out to the

cheese wheel, heads held high. When they heard the big white cat, they covered their eyes and began to pray, certain they would disappear, hiding them from the evil cat. This time was different. There was no noise. There was no screeching or meowing, only a deep and sinister laugh. This laughter began to rumble and became louder and louder until the cat was hysterical with laughter. The lead rat, full of himself and self-righteous in his faith, decided to open his eyes and yelled, "how dare you mock me! I am of the faithful rats!" He saw the big white cat looking down at him. The rat told his friend to open his eyes as he was of the faithful and nothing would happen to him. The friend opened his eyes and immediately, in front of the lead rat, the cat picked his friend up by the tail and devoured him. The rat strong in faith did not flinch. He rebuked the cat, who began laughing hysterically once again. The cat then yelled, "shut up!" Then the cat began telling the story from his perspective.

He explained to the rat, the first time he came out so skinny and scared that when he saw him, the cat didn't even want to eat him. So he decided to fatten the rat up and eventually eat him. He told the rat he was such a desperate looking rat at that time it wasn't worth his while. "But then," the cat said, "the next day you came out and brought your friends." So he watched as all the rats covered their eyes and began to pray. The cat told the rat that it was at that point he decided to make a lot of noise like he was chasing rats around. And after making a little noise he just plucked two of the rats and ate

them, "leaving you and a few alive in order to bring
more rats back and make my job that much easier."
"So see? The entire time I could see you, and you
brought your brothers and sisters for me to devour.
Meanwhile, you have become fat. You are so fat that
you can't even run from me if I wanted to eat you.
And now, I have eaten all of your brothers and
sisters. You have become so dependent on the food I
provide to you, wrapped up in your false beliefs,
that you don't even remember or desire to provide
for yourself."

The rat began to feel low like he had done a bad
thing. It was at this point that the cat said to the rat,
"But see my friend, I did not eat you. You provided
for me and I provided for you. Those rats never
treated you as well as I treated you. You were
starving when you were dealing with the rats and
now you have an entire room and wall to yourself,
and all the food you can eat." The rat asked the cat,
"so I am your friend?" The cat replied, "of course
you're my friend. I would never let any other rat
harm you. I will always provide the best for you."
Then the cat asked the rat to do the same for him.
Happy to reciprocate the friendship, the rat asked
how he can help. The cat said to the rat, "in the other
wall there are many more rats that you have never
met before, teach them about your faith. Tell them
of the sacrifices your friends made and tell them of
the rebelliousness of the rats who uncovered their
eyes. Introduce yourself as The Rat Who Covers His
Eyes. The rats will listen to you because you have
become fat off the food I provide and they are

skinny, desperate and starving. Your plump and affluent appearance will impress them. Lead them to me and I will provide for you." The cat told the rat this is the **CIVIL...** thing to do and I have **RIGHTS** to eat while I'm feeding you. The Rat Who Covered His Eyes looked the cat square in the eyes, and agreed...

## *"The Entrepreneur"*

*The solitude and serenity of a home at 3:00 am for an entrepreneur is overshadowed by the noise of mental wheels engaged. Silence so still a pin drop could wake the neighbors. But that silence is deafening to the man that must kill what he and his family eats. And he by the essence of his nature would have it no other way.*

*-Riyaad Giovanni*

## Chapter 2 An Unjust Law

*"An unjust law is itself a species of violence. Arrest for its breach is more so." - Mahatma Gandhi*

We must understand the REVOLUTIONARY of yesterday has become the COON of today, even if it wasn't done so purposefully. A BLACK LEADER without an ECONOMIC STRATEGY is worse than a KLANSMEN WITH AN ECONOMIC STRATEGY. Our DISENFRANCHISEMENT is one of WEALTH disparity NOT civil rights. I remember reading *How to win Friends and Influence People,* arguably at one time the greatest book for our economy or at least for our economy's sales markets. But as I matured in thought I realized this book never addresses the realities of the Black economic situation. It is still a great book, but maybe one that should be delegated to pastors, librarians, and fast food clerks. Perhaps it should be turned into a historical reference as the definitive source for American sales and marketing techniques between 1960-2000.

Today's business is black and white, and as cut and dry as a firing squad. Very much in the same manner, as the inhabitants of James Town had to learn, "You work! You eat!", modern Black Americans have to learn the same lesson. Within a capitalistic society, one must either generate wealth externally through taxes, job creation, infrastructure development, etc., or one's person must become the product. To give an

Economic Dependence

example, the number of prisoners has increased 100 fold since the early 1900s[1]. In fact, America houses over half of the entire world's prisoner population. It is common knowledge that the statistical majority

---

[1] www.bjs.gov/content/pub/pdf/Pi94.pdf

of those prisoners are Black men[2]. These Black men were shepherded into the prison through policies and laws scripted for the sole purpose and intent of long-term wealth building for White America.

Yes, the United States is so diabolical that its business leaders have found a way to generate revenue from Black men exclusively sitting in prison. This is the reality of where we are as a community and sub-culture within this country. We have come full circle as a displaced people. In the business arena, it is evident that we are mimicking ancient Roman society and the great amphitheatres of lore, where a "thumbs up" meant life and a "thumbs down" meant death. Every day governments create "thumbs up" or "thumbs down" laws that take away from our liberties; laws that further disenfranchise its Black citizens. Laws that further relegate Black people to second-class citizens.

The sad part is we, the Black citizenry, are readily accepting of this relegation by living in a consumerist daze. We are drunk and high on consumerism. We have lost all-purpose and thought of being leaders in this world. We are simply sheep to be slaughtered and exploited. Consumable and non-rechargeable batteries to be sucked dry and tossed away. We are human fodder. We have no one but ourselves to blame for falling to this depth.

In some instances we are worse off mentally

---

[2] http://www.naacp.org/pages/criminal-justice-fact-sheet

presently than during slavery. At least during slavery we had a sense of production, creating something useful from nothing. We had hope for our future and a consistent work ethic for building something for future Black generations. This concept has all but died in Black people.

We must begin to think of ourselves almost as imprisoned gladiators. The potential to be great is there! We need to be broken down to the essence of who we are. There is a Chinese proverb that states, "the straw that does not serve to break the

back only serves to strengthen the warrior." Gladiators prowled the arena, light of foot determined to do one thing, survive! The Gladiator cherished each moment of life and trained and fought with a purpose. The Gladiator became the champions of Roman society. The Gladiator brought fame and fortune or gloom and doom to their benefactor. This mentality is the one we should take on, no...we <u>must</u> take on, because believe you me, just as the Gladiators entered the arena against the odds fighting wild beasts and outnumbered, they came out victorious and so can we. If we do not begin to change our hearts and minds, Black society will become the great Roman society that spawned the ideas of the Gladiator, no longer existing but remembered. Langston Hughes, Paul Robeson, Malcolm X, Martin King, Tennessee Williams, will be but whispers of a forgotten past that is our culture. Our history in this country will only be remembered as fuel for the fire of our own self-destruction.

*"The Distance"*

*The distance between success and myself can be immeasurable.  Even if my fingertips grasp opportunity, my eyes have to be able to discern what is being held.*

-Riyaad Giovanni

# Chapter 3 Unto Thine Self Be Known

*"I grew up like a neglected weed - ignorant of liberty, having no experience of it." - Harriet Tubman*

Before one can master anything, one must first master self. But in order to master self, one must know self. Thus, one should know where their capabilities begin and where they end. This is the hardest thing to swallow in life, looking in the mirror and telling your very soul where it is lacking; being honest with self and truly own one's shortcomings and bad habits. A place to begin is having a serious sit down with those whom you have a long-term relationship with, such as your relatives, friends, or past and present management. Even if you have burned a bridge in the past, rebuild that bridge in order to make yourself a better and more effective person. Begin to have a serious dialogue about your shortcomings and faults. Allow those you engage in this conversation to be as direct as possible, all the while you should be grateful and humbled by such loyalty and honesty.

Once you've opened up to this type of scrutiny, you will see that others who have remained in your life and by your side have displayed an immense amount of loyalty to you. You should return that loyalty with gratitude. You should fight with every ounce of self-control you have inside of you, the urge to defend yourself. Just sit and listen and take notes. Once you have polled your group regarding different aspects of your life, you should have compiled

a detailed list of what areas you are lacking; where you're overbearing, weak, shortsighted, or unknowledgeable. Like I stated previously, this will probably be the most difficult thing you will have to do in life; to kill your own ego and pre-conceived notions, ideologies and lies you have told yourself about yourself, and begin to build a revised self-image.

From experience I can tell you it will feel as though a death has occurred. If you do this with all honor and integrity intact, be prepared for a phoenix to rise from the ashes. Be prepared to turn those weaknesses into strengths, tactics, and techniques that will help you develop a new you. You'll have a new outlook and a new willingness to sacrifice for goals that may not come to fruition in your lifetime. This fight we are fighting as Black people is a generational fight. We must remember to remain steadfast with the idea that "I may not reap the seed I sow." The benefit of your sacrifice may be reaped by future generations.

But how do you turn a weakness into a strength, tactic or technique? Below is a mental fight chart I have developed to help you do just that. In the chart are examples to follow in order to gain insight. You can also replace your weaknesses with your strengths in this chart to identify how your positives can be used against you, causing you to lose opportunities.

## TABLE 1.1
## Fight Chart: Weaknesses

| Weakness | Work against self | Neutralize | Work for self |
|---|---|---|---|
| Lack of confidence | In competition or negotiations I can be bullied into submitting or giving up more than what would normally be necessary | I am overly prepared for all meeting. I will lead the conversation and stick to the points I know the best. I will be reluctant to give the floor to another speaker etc. | I allow my lack of confidence to slightly show in order for the competitor negotiator to become overly confident and cocky. In doing so, they will give too much information or their arrogance will cause them to not give enough information. At this point I can go on the attack and this will throw my competition off balance while I go in for the kill. |
| I Talk too much | Talk myself out of an opportunity. I bore the opportunity with unnecessary information. I give the competition | Stick to the point in the event it is necessary to speak. Speak to parties involved like they know everything you know. Don't explain anything | Give great detail about the most important facts the opportunity wants. You can do this by sending a form before negotiations or during negotiations to |

| | | | |
|---|---|---|---|
| | too much information. And that information is used against myself or my company. | in detail unless the parties ask for a greater understanding or explanation. | have the opportunity explain what is most important to them. |
| I am a hot head | Over react during negotiations. Mistake body nuances and gestures and interpret them in a negative manner. Make enemies and develop a reputation as someone who cannot conduct proper meetings or negotiations. | I can neutralize being a hot head by focusing my energy on taking notes and gaining insight and understanding of what is being conveyed. I can remove myself from being the front line negotiator and instead be there to listen and give insight. | Develop a reputation as a no-nonsense businessperson. Skip formalities and go straight to the point. Don't waste time with unnecessary discussions. |

TABLE 1.2

## Fight Chart: Strengths

| Strength | Work for self | Neutralize | Work against self |
|---|---|---|---|
| Personable | Obviously people will gravitate to me. They will be keen to listen to what I have to say. It will be easy to gain access to top level meetings. Easy to develop relationships | My opponent or opportunity can neutralize this strength by having someone just as personable as me leading the charge for them. | Stick to only the pertinent information. Make the meetings strictly about the numbers. Allow me to speak about unimportant topics that do not relate to the topic at hand. Give a false sense of a developing opportunity. Hard-line negotiations. |
| Highly educated | I am an authority. I show a commitment to accomplishment | Present someone just as knowledgeable. | Dumb down the conversation. Stress the importance of real life hard work. Make the conversation a blue collar conversation. Give the false sense that my |

|  |  |  | education has caused me to be an elitist. Give the false sense that I am philosophical and not a doer. |
|---|---|---|---|
| Fearless | Not scared to go after any opportunity or speak to any level person to win an opportunity. | Present a conservative front. | Present me in a reckless capacity. Show the importance of being prudent and skeptical about things. Present very conservative business models in order to throw me off balance and give into demands. |

Once self has been dissected, re-imagined and rebuilt, at this point the businessperson has an opportunity to possess the artistry of business advancement. There is no quick way to develop savvy business skills. One must be willing to learn throughout life, never giving up the position of student, never being above gaining new insights or methods, whoever or whatever the source maybe. Shut your mouth and open your eyes and ears.

Once you've thoroughly self assessed your strengths and weakness'. Here are 10 key points to keep your entrepreneurial/Business mind sharpened and focused.

1. Any and every mistake you stumble across is inching you closer to your own greatness.

2. Always be sure about what you're doing and with whom you're doing it.

3.
No obstacle is great enough to stop change or progress from happening.

4. It is not always the one who sets their sights on being the largest (or greatest) that ends up being the most useful.

5. Hard work and sacrifice are magical bedfellows that help you along your way to fame.

6. Focusing on ideas that have already been conceived allow you (and your audience) to miss out on creating something exciting and new.

6. Prosperity requires a team to do what it takes to reach the top.

8. Don't always be so eager (or loud) to share your ideas with the masses.

9. Being given something easily leaves one unfulfilled, whereas working for it satisfies the soul.

10. Never lie to yourself, your colleagues, your customers and you'll never have to defend yourself against negativity.
Every leader must possess certain basic qualities if they wish to skillfully lead. The following essential

qualities must be mastered through experience and maturity:

**LOYALTY**

**COURAGE**

**BENEVOLENCE**

**WISDOM**

**STERNESS**

It is rare that a person will find short cuts to developing these qualities without paying a hefty

price. Nevertheless, these qualities must be learned in pursuit of your conquest to the top. You may have to accept the fact that you have flaws, and will need to work everyday to become a better businessperson than you were the day before.

Not everyone's definitions for these five qualities are the same. But for the purpose of this book, I will keep the meanings as general as possible. <u>Loyalty</u> in any circumstance must remain at a constant. Even if the only person you need to remain loyal to is yourself, don't sell yourself short or "sell out". Don't allow your morals and values to be pushed aside for uncertainty. Loyalty to those that reciprocate in today's world of business is without a doubt diminishing. It is of the upmost importance that your word remains true, no matter the outcome. You see it in the predominately white corporate world everyday where someone that holds a certain type of authority promises another person a particular opportunity and completely reneges on their word, for whatever reason, and often without explanation. No matter the type of business you may venture into, loyalty to those you do business with (i.e. partners, vendors, employees, customers) cannot be stressed enough.

For those businesspersons wanting to open a business(s), deciding to foster a business in this capitalist society takes a great deal of <u>courage</u>. And just as with anything that has the possibility to give a great return, obstacles will manifest. As a businessperson, you mustn't coward away from being told No; you mustn't fear financial struggle; you mustn't fear not being accepted by the white business realm! The purpose of this book, as stated in the Forward message, is to break free from the shackles of white economy. You may very well have the book thrown at you and initially denied opportunities, but you must persevere. Have the courage to decline the opportunity to cater to non-Black people because the money may come easier and faster. Instead, be steadfast in your part of building the Black economy...it will come with many woes that you may not see the benefit of in your lifetime. Even if your position is one of authority working for another's company, have the courage to suggest taking business to the Black community.

In order to develop something that is not of the norm, one must understand that much will be given away for free; charity. Developing a true, working state of existence takes not only time, but also <u>benevolence</u>. Not every product, service, offering etc., can be capitalized on in these beginning stages. Black people have to be re-educated on the quality they are entitled to as consumers, hence marketing and public relations. Included in a healthy economic state is caring for the less fortunate. Be charitable in the way of giving other qualified Black people opportunities, even if your position is with a company that's not your own. This is how it is done in so many other communities, especially the white business community. If you work for a large company now, if you take a look at the middle and upper management, you will see the pattern of connection between the individuals. The old saying "it's not what you know, it's who you know" is absolutely true.

<u>Wisdom</u> is acquired over space and time. It can't be taught or mimicked. It is required to make

solid, productive decisions in the business world. Wisdom is finding inspiration in the most likely and unlikeliest of places. Knowing when to seize the moment and when to sit back and observe. Many people will always have an opinion about how you should do your business; take it for what it is, advice. Use that advice if it benefits your business, your community cause. The age of an individual does not always dictate the amount of wisdom they have. For some it takes one time to make a mistake to learn the lesson in it; for others, they have to hit their head a few times before it resonates. Now which of the two do you suspect are the wiser?

After you've determined the path to take in building your business or reputation in the Black community, stick with it unless wisdom or commonsense dictates otherwise. You will find resistance from many directions. Be unyielding to the unknown, to your competition, to those that can't see your vision. Without a stern stance by Black businesspersons to reinvent the neighborhoods with new businesses leading to more jobs, better housing, more advanced schools, our community will continue to collapse onto itself.

The company one chooses to keep is often an indicator of a person's character. This leads us to the axiom "birds of a feather flock together". If your desire is to be recognized as a person with strength, you must surround yourself with strong people. Choosing the right kind of people to interact with is a matter that's not to be taken lightly. The first impression that one often gets of who is a businessperson, is seeing the people around that businessperson. If competent and loyal people surround you, then others will likely consider you competent, loyal and wise. If the people around you are of opposite character, one can form an unfavorable opinion. The mistake that is often made is choosing the wrong organization to represent or choosing someone of low moral character and position to be mentored by or cohort with. Discipline and Morale must be apparent in the cohort group. Discipline is not a form of suppression, it's the character expected from businesspersons of high social and moral standards. It will allow the group to never deviate away from order, or those business principles of honor and integrity to hold and reign true.

You should never condone the lack of discipline or morale. The lack of discipline or morale is a contagious disease that leads to destruction. The greater position of responsibility, the greater the discipline and morale required from that individual. Discipline and morale does not mean the loss of individuality, it's the building of character, principles, and integrity! Certain luxuries may come along with the privilege of becoming a player in the Global Markets, but comfort and relaxation is not included amongst those luxuries. Once you become involved in the international business world, your problems don't decrease they actually multiply. You should always be aware of the three things:

(1) A possible conspiracy from within your own organization to overthrow/undermine your efforts.

(2) Both known and unknown enemies and competitors plotting your demise.

(3) The main destructive factors in the human psychology that have been associated with the downfall of many are Arrogance, Aggression and Greed.

## "No"

*The first utterance understood, "NO", placed a ceiling above expectation.*

*Though I must walk, No.*

*Though I must talk, No.*

*Though I must learn, No.*

*May I? No. Can I? No. Will you? No.*

*But I relished my desert.*

*My spirit refused!*

*Every fiber of my being utterly rejected the notion that I must live in subjugation.*

*That I must follow another's agenda, path, plan...life!*

*That I must accept No. That I must become intimate with No. That for every No, I am closer to a yes, what hog-wash.*

*I relish in my desert. So I turn No into my dinner and feast.*

*Sometimes dinner is a sandwich and other times it is a 10 course meal, but I endure. I endure because No is a condiment in my life and I dine on whatever plate is placed before me until I am able to relish in my desert.*

*Yes!*

*-Riyaad Giovanni*

## Chapter 4 If It's Luxury You Seek

*"I only gave voice to words of freedom and brotherhood, words they couldn't accept. Just words." - Patrice Lumumba*

Under most circumstances people will hear of you before they've been afforded the luxury of meeting you. Therefore, as they say, your reputation precedes you. You must guard it by any means necessary because it's the foundation of your power. This is why in the political arena candidates always attempt to discredit one another by attacking their opponent's reputation. An impeccable reputation can open the doors to unlimited opportunities before you've had the chance to commit one act or speak one word!

There are mirrors for the face, but none for the heart and mind. It is a must for a leader to know the hearts and minds of his men. Occasionally, people must be tested to prove their loyalty. Loyal is the one who delivers the bad news. Disloyal is the

41

one who fails to deliver the bad news. Here are a couple other tactics that may prove whether or not the people around you are useful to you: (1) Entrust them with money, to see if they will steal, to test their honesty. (2) Tell them a supposed secret, to test their confidentiality. Many people spend their time learning the lyrics to songs, when they should be learning the hearts and minds of those they have around them everyday. Essentially whomever you keep close company with you are entrusting with your life. You expect them to react to danger in the same way you would, not putting you into additional harm.

Keep your friends close and your enemies even closer. The reason this is said is because you want to be able to keep your eyes on your enemies to know what they're thinking and doing. As long as you can see them, they are far less harmless than they are out of your sight. With that in mind, you should be wary of friends. They are always around you and your possessions and often times easily aroused to jealousy and envy; therefore, they have the potential to betray you more quickly. Just because someone claims to be your friend, does not automatically qualify them has a loyal member to your cause. Often times individuals that you meet in the beginning or before your journey as a successful businessperson will be the loyal ones. This is because they are on a similar path. They believe in what you are trying to accomplish and understand the demands of such a journey. Remember, it was Brutus who betrayed Caesar, it was Judas who betrayed Jesus, and it was Sammy the Bull who betrayed Gotti! So trust no one completely! Money, Power, and Sex, are always sources of hatred. Unfortunately, these are three things that men and women are motivated by. Once you obtain any of those mentioned above, both friend and foe alike will wish for your demise or downfall. In the movie Scarface, immediately after Tony had Frank killed, he went to claim his woman and take over his drug empire. Although that was a fictional story, it occurs in everyday life without fail. History doesn't lie, and it often repeats itself.

Paranoia shouldn't be how you live your everyday life, but neither should you be naïve. Since this is a proven fact, a skilled leader should take up heavily in their study of world history, military science, and politics. The serious study of the past provides us with the insight needed for wise decision making for today and tomorrow. You must study the victories and defeats of those leaders who engaged in great wars in the past. Sometimes we have the tendency to make the same mistakes as those who came before us, so we must adopt those stratagems that have already been proven to be successful. John Quincy Adams said, "I must study wars and politics, so that my son can have the liberty to study mathematics and philosophy."[3] When someone thinks more of luxury than they do

---

[3]

www.masshist.org/digitaladams/archive/doc?id=L17800512jasecond

of war, they usually lose their wealth. Weak and wealthy is the worst of all. Because the wealthy will attract the attention of those with the will-power to take it from them. Historical fact, it was the Barbarians that defeated the Romans...

## "Invictus"

*Out of the night that covers me,*
*Black as the pit from pole to pole,*
*I thank whatever gods may be*
*For my unconquerable soul.*

*In the fell clutch of circumstance*
*I have not winced nor cried aloud.*
*Under the bludgeonings of chance*
*My head is bloody, but unbowed.*

*Beyond this place of wrath and tears*
*Looms but the Horror of the shade,*
*And yet the menace of the years*
*Finds and shall find me unafraid.*

*It matters not how strait the gate,*
*How charged with punishments the scroll,*
*I am the master of my fate,*
*I am the captain of my soul.*

-William Ernest Henley

# Chapter 5 Emotionalism is the Death of Building

*"Speak when you are angry and you will make the best speech you will ever regret."*
— *Ambrose Bierce*

You must learn to control your emotions instead of letting your emotions control you. Always try to take the rational approach to a problem, rather than the emotional approach. A state of balance and harmony means an attitude that is not affected by emotions. Love is dangerous, because it blinds the eyes. Anger is destructive, because it clouds the judgment. Under no circumstance are your emotions to play a role in planning or decision-making. It should be business, never personal. Business doesn't have emotions, only profits and losses! This may seem contradictory and counter to doing business with Black people and creating Black wealth, but it is not. One should not forgo good business for the cause of attempting to be inclusive of black economics. Instead one should impeccably conduct business in order to up

the standards of black people while simultaneously
laying a strong structural foundation that will stand
the tests of time. Break down the oppression of
white supremacy while increasing Black
understanding and determination.

Most people are totally unaware when they
make an enemy. A wise man makes enemies
intentionally, not by accident. When you insult
someone, you should mean it. Challenging a
person's esteem and security and not be willing to
deal with the consequences of doing so, can be a
grave mistake. Even an arch coward will defend his
honor and dignity if he is disrespected in public.
Wars usually don't begin when one force is
aggressive toward the other, they usually begin
when one force speaks aggressively towards the

other. You cannot go to war and make money at the same time. During times of peace, you must prepare yourself financially for war. ASSETS, PROFITS, CASH ON HAND, and LAWYER FEES must be at your immediate disposal. If you don't have access to any of these things in the heat of the moment, I suggest you avoid wars with entities that do.

Never bring business home. Whatever happens outside the home stays outside the home. One should only bring home information on a need to know basis. Remember, your home is your family's sanctuary from the outside world! A good business-person strives to maintain a balance between work and family, with family always coming first. After all the purpose of building wealth is to bolster our families. If you want to share your business with your family do it during business hours and at the business facilities. If you are a person that conducts business from home, separating business from family life can be even more difficult. But you must work even harder to create distinction between workspace and family space, work time and family time. Ultimately, there is nothing more important than parenting. This comes before profits, losses, your business plan and strategies. Always keep this in the forefront of your mind. A strong family can help you develop and hone leadership skills. A good family life can also help de-stress and clarify one's business world.

### "untitled"

*when shall your wounds
welcome their scabs?*

*daily your kingdom squeaks
and leaps to the starlight*

*it wants all of you
you of all and the music*

*of the pastures of midnoon
a little boy's kaleidoscopticon*

*you are the one the music
has chosen and whom strings call*

*twilight moans behind you
all you are you are all*

*it is the boy in black talking
how civil is the civil war?*

*-Uche Nduke*

## CHAPTER 6 Fair is Fair! So be Fair

*"What a country needs to do is be fair to all its citizens - whether people are of a different ethnicity or gender." - Chinua Achebe*

Unfortunately, there may come a time when you have to mediate a problem between subordinates within your immediate circle. It is your responsibility as a leader to make sure things

run smoothly amongst your team. It's extremely important that all problems are resolved as quickly and decisively as possible, before any relationships get beyond repair. It is my suggestion, that you sit both individuals down together and have them discuss the situation. Direct unfiltered communication serves to elevate stress. It gives an individual a since that they are valued as well as relevant within your business. Lastly, direct communication empowers and builds loyalty. It gives your team a feeling they are a part of the decision making process. If direct communication proves itself to be unsuccessful and the parties cannot talk their problems out, then a good leader does not hesitate to become the judge and jury, rendering a resolution to the issue.

Niccolo Machiavelli stated, "it's better to be feared, than to be loved."[4] I find that to be true because men are governed by fear and nothing else. Men will love you at their own will, but they will fear you at your will. This is the basis of white supremacy and the current state of our economy. But this doesn't have to be our paradigm. We can create a new paradigm that love and loyalty are the sentiments of the day. We can create a paradigm that battles the harsh cold world of western economics by using the same tactics that white supremacy has used to enclose us into an economically disadvantaged box. We can create fear through economic cohesion and spending. This should be the battle cry of every black leader, and conscious or self-actualized person striving to make a difference either in your personal life, family, community or the world.

---

[4] The Prince by Nicolo Machiavelli CHAPTER XVII

Dr. Riyaad Giovanni

A wise leader must rely on things he can control. Fear is established and maintained through the certainty of the administering of a dreadful punishment. This is how white society has maintained a strong hold over the minds of Black people. This is how white supremacy has become so embedded in the minds of Black people. Being righteous not callus, being benevolent not miserly, developing loyalty, not allegiance and cultivating love instead of fear should be the precursors in our establishment and ultimately the success and independence we stand on when pulling away from this white westernized economic mechanism. It's because of these newly developed altruistic business tactics alone that both peers and competitors will undoubtedly learn to respect us. They will know that any form of plot or disrespect will guarantee their own destruction!

A great leader must maintain a healthy mind and a healthy body. There can never be enough emphasis placed on this point. One must reframe from Alcohol and Drugs. These are two destructive vices that have a physical and psychological effect on the human body. You must also partake in some form of an exercise regimen, have a well balanced diet, and get the proper rest. A clear and focused mind and a well-conditioned body must work in cohesion with each other. All of these factors will play a crucial role in your ability to make sound and logical decisions. You must have sincere and genuine concern for the welfare of your team and their families. You never want to be perceived as being selfish and stingy. You must share the spoils of successful business, thus increasing the love, and decreasing the hate.

There are two forms of hatred. One is internal, and one is external. The latter refers to outside powers and can be defended by arms and allies. An internal hatred refers to the conspiracies of subordinates to overthrow you. Conspiracies are motivated by three of the following things: HATRED, GREED, and JEALOUSY. These traits can be guarded against by being loved by those who are surrounding you. If they love you and are loyal, they will protect you.

### "The Eye"

*Said the Eye one day, "I see beyond these valleys a mountain veiled with blue mist. Is it not beautiful?"*

*The Ear listened, and after listening intently awhile, said, "But where is any mountain? I do not hear it."*

*Then the Hand spoke and said, "I am trying in vain to feel it or touch it, and I can find no mountain."*

*And the Nose said, "There is no mountain, I cannot smell it."*

*Then the Eye turned the other way, and they all began to talk together about the Eye's strange delusion. And they said, "Something must be the matter with the Eye."*

*-Khalil Gibran*

## Chapter 7 Your Leadership is Only as Credible as Your Personal Life

*"Do not go where the path may lead, go instead where there is no path and leave a trail."*
*- Ralph Waldo Emerson*

It's mandatory a leader live by strict codes and ethics. Never shedding the cloak of honor, morality,  or dignity. Leaders will forever be under a big microscope, their actions constantly being studied and scrutinized. No two things will cause you more problems than the flesh between your jaws, and the flesh between your legs. If you can control those two things, 95% of your problems will be nonexistent. Always remain calm, even in the midst of chaos. Maintain self-discipline while staring in the eyes of temptation, and stand firm during moments of challenge and adversity. All great people have led by example. You are the epitome of what your men should strive to be. Never try to accomplish by force what can be accomplished through negotiations. Sun Tzu said, "Weapons are an evil omen, and any use of force should be your final alternative. Diplomacy is a method that's used by men, while the use of arms is that of beasts."[5] The techniques of negotiations are not easily taught. They are mastered only through understanding, gained by experience.

The following is a short list of do's and don'ts when it comes to negotiations: (1) Always maintain the diplomatic initiative in all negotiations. Be on the offensive always. This will place the other party at a disadvantage and give you the upper hand. (2) Enter negotiations armed with knowledge of your party's strengths and weakness. Knowing this will give you the advantage and allow you to better deceive him of your ultimate goals (deception will be a must when dealing with the larger white economy as the powers that built that evil institution will work tirelessly to strip down and destroy any semblance of Black unity attempting to set up a black first economy). (3) Keep negotiations secret. They must be conducted in private with only the necessary parties involved. This will save you

---

[5] The Art of War by Tsun Tzu Jeff McNiell Classics, LLC, 2012

loss of face in the event things don't work out in your favor. (4) Never arbitrate. Arbitration allows a third party to determine your destiny. Only the weak use an arbitrator.

(5) Honor all agreements made during negotiations. Be a person of your word, and this will make you more respected in the eyes of your enemies. You must learn to use deception as a means of keeping your enemies off balance. When you are weak you must appear to be strong. When you are broke you must appear to be rich. Your enemies will look for signs of weakness, and try to attack you at a time when they feel you're most vulnerable.

No one must ever obtain the inner secrets of your circle. You must do everything in your power to gather intelligence on your enemies. Knowledge about your enemies cannot be gotten from ghost or spirits, it must be obtained from people that know the conditions, habits, and thoughts. Remember the white business world is set on you being a second class, under paid, non-wealth having member of their working class. Machiavelli said, "you either caress your enemies or annihilate them, or injure them to the point where you fear not his vengeance."[6] This is very clear' there are no grey areas here. You never want to give your enemy a chance to regroup and come back to challenge you another day if at all possible. Revenge is a dish that's served cold! Nothing will please your enemies

---

[6] The Prince by Nicolo Machiavelli CHAPTER XVII

more than to repay you for an injury once suffered at your hands.

### *"Be King of Circumstance"*

*...Though black of race you are, my friend,*

*Your part in life is ever here:*

*There's work for you; the human trend*

*Calls for each one to have his share.*

*Go then and play your part to-day,*

*And think that you are king of all*

*Circumstances that come your way.*

*Before which you must never fall.*

*-Marcus Garvey*

## Chapter 8 Use Logical Law and Order

*"You deserve to be slaves." - Denmark Vesey*

There cannot be order without laws. As a leader, you must establish a set of by-laws that everyone must adhere to and abide by. Violators of the law must be subject to some form of disciplinary action. This will keep your team united and loyal. When disciplinary action is taken, it will injure an individual. When disorder or disloyalty arises, it will injure everyone. It is a must to show no favoritism when handing down sanctions. No one individual is bigger than the whole team. A person's worth is not determined by individual accomplishments. Value rest solely upon

demonstrated support of the goals that are sought in order to achieve as a collective unit. The spirit of unity, loyalty, discipline, and moral are cardinal principles that must be instilled in all. The greatest human endeavor is when a group of people work together for a common cause.

The first thing that should be established whether in a leadership position or not, is a clear understanding of logic. One of the fastest ways to derail talks, communications, action, forward movement, and progress is by allowing illogical thoughts, influences and arguments to be introduced. Best case scenario is illogical infusions into the stream of consciousness of a situation will result in a temporary sidetrack. The worst-case scenario is a complete hindrance to progress and a combative situation.

So we must begin to understand basic Logic and how to identify a logical and illogical statement. There are four principles/rules of reason (logic):

First Rule of logic

(1) The Principle of Identity - A thing is what it is for example an airplane is an airplane. It is not a car, nor a train.

(2) The Principle of the Excluded Middle - Between being and non-being there is no middle. Something either exists or it doesn't. There is no middle ground between existing and nonexistent.

(3) The Principle of Sufficient Reason - There is a sufficient reason for everything. Everything that is

in the physical world has an explanation for existing.

(4) The Principle of Contradiction - It is impossible for something to be and not be at the same time and in the same respect. For example, you can not be at work and at the same time physically be across town at your child's dance recital or soccer game.

Although some may argue you can be at work physically and simultaneously be mentally at your child's activity. This is why "in the same respect" is of the utmost importance in the statement of The Principle of Contradiction. It is very important to study and truly understand logic for the purpose of staying away form absolute statements that create impossible parameters and creates distrust when made. An example is if you tell a family member, "I would never lie to you." Well what about Santa Clause, The Easter Bunny or "No honey, the extra weight gain looks good on you". Although these are comical examples, lets see how these type absolute statements can truly damage a relationship or understanding. When an employee interviewing for a job makes a statement like "I'm never late for work or miss work." Or if the employer makes a statement like we value your work output and judge you solely based on your performance. But at the same time the company has seniority incentive program in place for promotions and job security.

Second Rule of logic

Real and manufactured gray areas - A gray area is a situation where the truth cannot be clearly established. Many people will waste your time and your efforts with constant "gray" area arguments and presentations. The only reason the gray area exists is because of the distinct black and white alternatives. Another situation we must keep in mind is that just because we find ourselves in gray area does not mean there are no clear black and white alternatives. So just because we may not be able to clearly see the black and white alternatives we should not project our subjectivity upon the world. If your solution to economic freedom is working for White America and you cannot see any other alternative to capital gains, then don't infect those Black people who have developed and are living an alternative lifestyle outside of working for White America. Better yet, do not infect those who are seeking an alternative to their current situation by making them feel it's impossible to make it without the assistance of White America.

## Third rule of Logic

Everything can eventually be explained. The Principle of Sufficient Reason once again makes it impossible for things to just happen. Everything that exists has a cause. Knowing this and truly understanding this will keep the looks of confusion off your face. You will constantly look for solutions instead of making excuses for something that clearly exists.

Fourth Rule of Logic

Don't stop short in the search for causes - Just because poor diet causes hypertension does not mean that stress isn't a cause of hypertension also. Had researchers stopped at poor diet being a cause and not continued to look for answers they would have never discovered stress as a cause for hypertension too.

Fifth Rule of Logic

Distinguish among causes - There are four distinct causes:

(1) The Efficient Cause - Is an agent that causes something into existence or modifies existence in some way.

(2) The Final Cause - This can be explained as the purpose of the activity.

(3) The Material Cause - The actual material out of which something is composed.

(4) The Formal Cause - The identifying nature of a thing, why it is what it is. For an example what makes a lamp a lamp and not a desk and vice versa?

Sixth Rule of Logic

Define your terms - Vagueness and ambiguity are killers of dialogue and following an argument to its ultimate conclusion. Therefore a clear definition of terms and understanding should be spelled out. When defining terms we relate it as rigorously as possible to the object to which it refers. Doing so leaves virtually no room for misunderstanding.

## Seventh Rule of Logic

The Categorical Statement - An argument is only as good as the statements that proceed it. A categorical statement tells us a definitive thing. For instance The White House is in Washington, D.C. as opposed to a non categorical statement which basically means a person is to take something at face value or just believe without proof. So an example of the opposite of a categorical statement would be "Black men are bad father's because all my friends children have Black father's and none of them are involved."

## Eighth Rule of Logic

Generalizing - A general statement is when the object being discussed is large in scope. Generalizing does not mean the statement is necessarily false. For example, humans are mammals. In this example, the assumption is that every single human male or female of every race is a mammal. If we are not wanting to explicitly express every scenario under which a human can exist, then we can say something like "and some humans are female". But because all humans are not female, we cannot say all humans or mammals are female. Now back to the "Black men are bad fathers" argument. This would be an inaccurate generalization because it's impossible for all Black fathers to be bad fathers. So we should stay away from making these types of statements if we want to stay within the constraints of logical arguments and discussion.[7]

---

[7] Being Logical: A Guide To Good Thinking D.Q. McInerny

*"Toussaint L'Ouverture"*


*To those fair isles where crimson sunsets burn,*
*We send a backward glance to gaze on thee,*
*Brave Toussaint! thou was surely born to be*
*A hero; thy proud spirit could but spurn*
*Each outrage on the race. Couldst thou unlearn*
*The lessons taught by instinct? Nay! and we*
*Who share the zeal that would make all men free,*
*Must e'en with pride unto thy life-work turn.*
*Soul-dignity was thine and purest aim;*
*And ah! how sad that thou wast left to mourn*
*In chains 'neath alien skies. On him, shame! shame!*
*That mighty conqueror who dared to claim*
*The right to bind thee. Him we heap with scorn,*
*And noble patriot! guard with love thy name.*


-Henrietta Cordelia Ray

67

## Chapter 9 Be the Guest in Times of War

*"You've got to have a villain and they'll always make me a villain. I'm used to it - it makes me work harder and it makes me fight harder." - Floyd Mayweather, Jr.*

Who are your real enemies? Who are your real friends? These are questions of great importance, because in times of war, you must unite with real

friends to attack real enemies. Strategically, you should despise all your enemies, but tactically, you must take them all seriously. Never underestimate any of them! White supremacy should be a system of business that is battled against every day of the rest of you life. However, use humility to make your enemies arrogant, and their arrogance will cause them to underestimate you. Underestimation will always lay the groundwork for a surprise attack, which should be swift and effective. In the world of business a surprise attack can be a timely product launch, an effective marketing campaign to rebrand and repackage a product. There are a few more questions that every skilled warrior must ask himself before engaging in battle. By answering these questions, you will determine your strengths and                                    weaknesses:

(1) Who is the wiser businessperson?
(2) Who is better prepared?
(3) Who is the more skilled?
(4) Who has more money, assets &
    cash on hand?
(5) Who is the bravest?
(6) Who has superior allies?

Tsun Tzu stated in The Art of War, "In war you should prefer to be the guest as opposed to being the host."[8] When you engage in combat in your

---

[8] The Art of War by Tsun Tzu Jeff McNiell Classics, LLC, 2012

enemy's territory, unlike him, you always have the option of retreating. If he fights at home, he has nowhere to run. But never forget, a concerned man becomes a desperate man. And a desperate man will resort to desperate measures as a means of survival. You must form a council of men that you can consult with and seek advice from. These men should be wise and capable of giving you their honest objective opinion. They should be free to speak the truth and you should be a patient hearer of the truth, with regards to the things you ask about and nothing more. Your council should not feel like they are at liberty to say whatever they want and lead to disrespect. They should also be at least 40 years of age. The age is significant because at 20 a person is ruled by their will, at 30 they are driven by their intellect, and at age 40 they have relatively sound judgment. Getting advice from the wise can be the distinction between victory and defeat, or life and death! In the movie Godfather III, Michael and Vincent traveled all the way to Sicily to consult with one of the older and wise Dons...

A wise business person must learn to emulate two animals, the fox and the lion. You'll need the courage of a lion to fight off your enemies, and you'll need the slyness of a fox to avoid traps laid by the enemy. Courage without intellect is a calamity waiting to happen. They must coexist together if one wishes to truly be successful. Nature has given the bee the sweetness of honey and the sharpness of its sting. Security is first and foremost. Nothing takes priority or precedence over security. Those around you must always be alert and prepared to deal with any situation that arises. Your enemies will be waiting for opportunities to catch you with your guard down. Regardless of how small a task may seem, exercise and proceed with caution at all times, Proper Preparation Prevents Poor Performance. Never overlook the possibility of hiring mercenaries to dispose of an enemy for you. This is a tactic that can be used as a decoy to divert the attention away from you. You never want to bring any unnecessary heat on yourself. However, be very careful when dealing with mercenaries, because the only thing that they're loyal to is money! A prime example of disposing of an enemy would be a paid negative ad campaign or paying a human rights organization to research the ethics of the business practices of your enemy.

## *"The Decision Sonnet"*

*The work world weighs on the manager's mind*
*What to do among so many answers*
*Facts, folly, invention, and hope intertwined*
*At stake are jobs, people, clients, and dollars*
*Choice is fear is chilling and a horror*
*The weak defer to willing surrogates*
*Then become inert and anemic leaders*
*Jeers to the managerial cheapskates*
*The lions of the workplace must rescue*
*Teams, their puny peers, and enterprise*
*Courage and strength can produce a breakthrough*
*Proactivity and strength make them wise*
*Decisions, while tough, are management metal*
*They build character, strength, trust and muscle.*

*- Lisa Haneburg*

## Chapter 10 Desire the Virtue of Patience

*"... no one can be given a gift greater than patience."- Muhammad Ibn Abdullah*

It's true what they say...patience is a virtue! You must never rush in your critical decision-making. Often times, a thorough investigation must be conducted in order to ascertain the facts surrounding a situation. You cannot hesitate to act, but neither can you prematurely make decisions that will work to your disadvantage. When the consequences of your decisions are too grim to bear, look for another option. Rarely are there perfect decisions. The best ones are usually the most logical ones. You must grow to understand that the wisdom of a particular decision can change with time. Make every effort to improve future decisions by learning from those you've already made. It is your peers that suffer the most when you excel. The greater your accomplishments, the greater the opposition, torment, and discouragement your enemies will throw in your path. Expect it, but don't become victim to it. Use it as a motivational tool to further your cause. When nothing is being said negatively about you that almost always means you probably haven't accomplish anything of great importance.

There are two kinds of wars, Just and Un-just. Wars that help you progress, are wars that are just. Wars that impede progression are wars that are un-just. Only go to war when it will further your cause. The object of war is to preserve self while destroying the enemy. To destroy the enemy means to disarm him, or deprive him of the power to resist. Disarming him doesn't necessarily mean physically attacking him. Cutting off your enemy's source of finance is a thousand times better than immobilizing his army. You should always be for peace, but not afraid of war. A wise warrior always thinks of war, whether it's preventing it or engaging in it. Never relax after victory because after enemies with ammunition have been wiped out, there will be enemies without ammunition!

At times it becomes necessary for you to replace your leadership. Do not fear this moment. This is a moment that should have been planned for a while. Do not choose the one with the most knowledge or the one with the most talent or the one most liked. Choose the one who undoubtedly understands how to lead and delegate authority and develop cohort groups. This is the most patient thing you can do as a business owner and it will take every bit of patients you have. This can never be an emotional decision and must be the best decision for the advancement and sustenance of the organization/company. Many times we wish to rush our children into these positions. This requires a thorough assessment of your children's abilities and talents as a leader and it also requires prior preparation. Do not feel the need to force your children into a leadership role. Make them earn it and do not become afraid of the possibility of bringing in a temporary leader to lead while your children mature in their leadership abilities.

Dr. Riyaad Giovanni

*"The Decision Haiku"*

*Oh, the angst of choice*
*Acid churning, can't think straight-*
*Big leap, then relief*

- Unknown

## Chapter 11 Our Struggle Against White NORMALITY

*"Liberate the minds of men and ultimately you will liberate the bodies of men." - Marcus Garvey*

Do you want to know why it seems so many

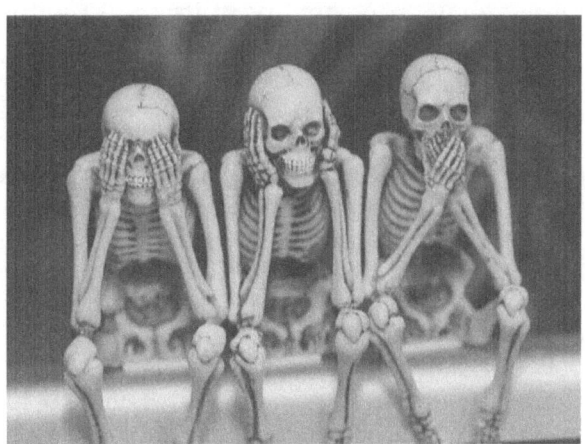

White people are having an adverse reaction to the Black movement for equality? Contrary to the popular mantra of "white supremacy" that so recklessly falls out the mouth of activist as often as misappropriated participles are in the speech of toddlers. The reason is simpler and more mundane in nature, white normality. Viewing the world with the understanding that the baseline of comprehension is that of the average white American is even more dangerous than Supremacy.

There is a clear cut evil in supremacy that one can take side against and convince the majority of people to fight against. And contrary to popular opinion few people are supremacist. The result of supremacist policies in America was the ending of slavery, de-segregation, jobs programs and much more (a white paradigm of equality). Truly for the most part white people put forth an effort to eradicate open and overt supremacist government but what they left behind was more sinister in nature. Because the governance and implementation of supremacy goes so far beyond the pale of human accepted behavior, normality in its covert nature of existence seems an acceptable alternative.

What normality really does is create a condition like unto supremacy in result over time. Without the harsh day-to-day wholesale mistreatments and abuses necessary to keep a subjugated people in check through fear. When my experience, knowingly different, is the experience from which laws are derived no matter how civilized the process. Then that process tells others being governed that their normal is abnormal. And let's be honest abnormal behavior is victimized, criminalized and institutionalized. The real issues are never forced to the forefront to be addressed by the "normal" majority. The "normal" majority most often does not realize the adverse effects it has on the "abnormal" minority groups they govern.

The result is allowing a supremacist like outcome without the overt feelings of institutional racism. BUT MAKE NO MISTAKE, WHITE NORMALITY IS WORSE THAN OPEN RACISM BECAUSE IT ALLOWS FOR THE SAME RESULTS OF SUPREMACY WITHOUT THE GUILT!

## "A Poem For All Entrepreneurs"

*The road to success is paved with tests,*
*So you've got to believe in yourself above the rest.*
*Dream big, and let your passion shine,*
*If you don't, you won't end up with a dime.*
*Challenge the status quo, disrupt the market and say*
*YES!*
*And remember that innovation is an endless quest.*
*Don't forget to change business for good,*
*If you want to change the world then you should.*
*If you think with your head and listen to your heart,*
*I promise you'll get off to a flying start.*
*Make bold moves, but always play fair,*
*Always say please and thank you – it's cool to care.*
*Do what you love and love what you do,*
*This advice is nothing new.*
*Now, stop worrying about whether your business will be*
*a hit,*
*Rise to the challenge and say 'screw it, let's do it!'*

*- Sir Richard Branson*

## Chapter 12 All Leadership Ain't Good Leadership

*"One of the most deadly causes of destruction is when a
leader is failing, but he or she does not know it. Ignorance
about your role is a death plot against people's
successes."* — *Israelmore Ayivor*

 Can you name one Black American leader
that has an
entire economic
end game on
paper ready to
be
implemented?
I'm tired of the
"come together"
people. I'm
talking about if
Black people
were given land
and sovereignty
today. What type of economy would we have
tomorrow? How would we take care of public
works, education, defense? What would doing

business look like? Would it be capitalism, socialism, communism, barter and trade or something else? Would speculating be allowed if not how would we back the money? If a resource based monetary system is the plan, then what resource? You should look for that Black person to throw your support behind. The one that has thought this situation through an end game not just sound bites to get black folks to throw support and money at the latest program being sold.

So many questions need to be addressed into a comprehensive model of what we want and need. How would we handle inflation, what matrix do we set up in order to measure growth. What role would government play? Total control or liaise fair? What about international trade? How would we handle imports? What about labor related issues, like employee pay?

It's already only a few black leaders talking money. But what Black leaders are truly talking and developing macro/micro economics?

A sickness I have come to understand more and more as of late. Black people fear Black people who do not have a healthy fear/reverence for white supremacy. A black leader without an economic strategy is almost as bad as the Klan. Where are you leading your followers? A better question is where are YOU being lead? Too many economics experts speak about economics but not family. Family is the foundation on which an economy is built. For most people a cohesive family can provide the seed money and employees needed to start a business. Family can also be the negativity that keeps you from ever trying. Most people do not qualify for and will not get the funds they need from loans and investors. If your listening to someone about economics that is not talking equally about family, then that person doesn't have a realistic grasp of the common man's situation.

Do you understand that economic empowerment is our underground railroad?! That consumerism and pay gap disparity is our slavery? This is for my generation and younger. We cannot go the way of the civil rights generations. I truly want you to understand the numbers. Although this study was completed in 2009 the numbers are tracking very similar today. In 2009, a representative survey of American households revealed that the median wealth of white families was:

- $113,149 compared...and $5,677 for black families.1

- Each $1 in income for white America yields $5.19 of growth.

- Each $1 in income for black American yields $0.69 of growth.

- Each $1 in inheritance for white America yields $0.91 of growth.

- Each $1 in inheritance for black America yields $0.20 of growth.[9]

In laymen's terms what does this data mean? Removing the work pay disparity and dealing strictly with income received. It speaks to Blacks ability to spend money on worthless "pop culture"

---

[9] https://www.ssa.gov/policy/docs/ssb/v64n4/v64n4p1.html

non-asset items. It speaks to Back peoples inability to be fiscally responsible. It speaks to the sheer failure of the older Black generation to live a virtuous debt free lifestyle. Black people willingly gave their money and time away for the appearance of middle class and the cost is leaving nothing behind. It speaks to Black peoples income mostly going to service debt and not to invest or schemes to increase income. It speaks to Blacks inability and lack of desire to circulate money with other Black people. And the most disheartening situation it speaks to is the older Black peoples' nonchalant attitude about leaving absolutely nothing behind to stabilize the family.

The selfishness of Black America - we live a lifestyle of limited self-indulgence financed with the future stability of our families. Older Black people have sold out future generations with their desire to be inclusive in white privilege. Older Black people have become complete consumers not knowing how to generate money beyond work in exchange for pay. If you are trying to develop an entrepreneurial mindset or are struggling to pull away from your job or your entrepreneurial effort isn't quite successful. I recommend you get rid of any Boogie or Civil Rights minded friends. Steer clear of these people. I also recommend that you steer clear of those Black people whom have had "some success" through advanced degrees and playing the American game. Their is a difference between being Free and being Kept. And this type of black bourgeoisie / leadership will convince you being kept is the same as being free.

The Rat That Covered Its Eyes: 11 Rules For A Post Civil Rights
Struggle


*Rule 1: An Unjust Law* - Always fight against an unjust law. In fact an
unjust law is nothing more than oppression.

*Rule 2: Unto Thine Self Be Known* - Never fall victim to delusions of
grandeur about self. Constantly asses yourself and make adjustment
that will be beneficial to yourself and society at large.

*Rule 3: If Its Luxury You Seek* - You will only reap the benefit of that
which you strive to obtain.

*Rule 4: Emotionalism Is The Death of Building* - A person that is not in
control of their emotional state is always at a disadvantage during
tough times.

*Rule 5: Fair Is Fair! So Be Fair!* - Simply put fair play and dealings is a
must. Your reputation depends on fair and honest dealings.

*Rule 6: Your leadership Is Only As Credible As Your Personal Life.* - Your
personal lifestyle is a reflection of who you are. If your personal life
is in shambles then most likely your business and public life is in
shambles or on its way there.

*Rule 7: Use Logical Law And Order* - This may be the most important
rule. Sound logical statement, arguments, ideas, communication and
strategies need to be assessed and applied in order to be successful.

*Rule 8: Be The Guest In Times Of War* - This rule is more metaphorical
but can have physical implications. Try not to paint yourself into a
corner where there is no room or ground to retreat to.

*Rule 9: Desire The Virtue Of Patience* - Patience is the gift that allows
perseverance through the struggle.

*Rule 10: Our Struggle Against White Normality* - Living life chasing the
White American paradigm of understanding is detrimental to black
society. We must create a world where our vision and understanding
is just as valid.

*Rule 11: All Leadership Ain't Good Leadership* - Our biggest failure
since Civil Rights has been the lack of accountability to which we
hold our black leaders. Raise the bar and make them accountable.

## Epilogue

The illusion of freedom has Black people in America thinking we're free when 97.5% of our household income is from white entrepreneurs or government benefits! I'm not telling you to quit your job today. I am trying to teach you how to create a job today so you can quit tomorrow. I try my best not to come off as negative and to provide realistic information that will give an understanding of the dynamic Black people are under in America. And to give some idea of what it will take to move us outside or from under the harshness of White normality. White America (meaning white entrepreneurs and tax dollars) employs 94% of black America. Under this white altruism, despite racism, we black folks then demand more jobs, more housing, more food stamps, more welfare etc. Despite the story of America being a melting pot. The fact is that the vast majority of white America views Americans in terms of race/ethnic groups. Knowing the above data we should be aware that our "black" demands can be viewed as ungratefulness or simply entitlements. Especially in light of racist rhetoric or a paradigm based in white normality. Simply because not only do we not provide for ourselves, but we fail to reciprocate economic gain other than self exploitation.

This situation could easily be combated if Black people in America created more jobs and reciprocated the employment of white Americans. But the 20+ million Black adults in America only create about 800,000 jobs and 600,000 of those jobs are staffed by Black people. In fact, we only reciprocate employment opportunities to white America at a rate of 100,000 to 15,000,000. That means for every job a Black entrepreneur offers a white person. A White person offers 150 Black people a job. Often times Black folks use the excuse that everyone can't be an entrepreneur. This is true. Knowing this fact does not absolve black people from investing, preparing, supporting, guiding and teaching future generations to be more independent and less dependent.

We can continue to march, yell at white people, talk about the inequalities of white normality and basically appeal to white America's already over altruistic manner. (This is a separate subject than reparations. White America must make amends). Make no mistake I am not absolving white America of the institutionally racist and oppressive institutions they have set up. But begging in the name of civil rights is irrelevant and defeatist. Economic stability is the only way to combat against institutional and exploitative government.

We sound like teenage children too irresponsible to truly know how life works arguing with our parents about being grown and wanting freedoms as black people. How can we be free when 94% of our income is derived from White America. As conscientious black people we have to take account of our weakness and put forth effort to be creators of business, institutions and industry. Once again, for the people that love to blame everything on racism, I am in no way limiting the impact or blame that should be placed on white normality/supremacy. I'm just attempting to shift the paradigm from one of victim to empowered.

In conclusion, People always ask me why I go so hard on economics and racial issues and the reason is because my daddy didn't and so my children won't have too. I truly believe younger people are getting it. I was smothered in white normality and culture growing up. I was made to feel the white way was the right/only way. I have to do everything I can to create space for my children to roam and dwell in free from niggers and white society oppressors so they can become the best of whom they choose to be. NOT what white society or broken "nigga's" have programmed them to be.

## *"Declaration of the Rights of the Negro Peoples of the World": The Principles of the Universal Negro Improvement Association/Marcus Garvey*

### *Preamble*

*Be It Resolved, That the Negro people of the world, through their chosen representatives in convention assembled in Liberty Hall, in the City of New York and United States of America, from August 1 to August 31, in the year of Our Lord one thousand nine hundred and twenty, protest against the wrongs and injustices they are suffering at the hands of their white brethren, and state what they deem their fair and just rights, as well as the treatment they propose to demand of all men in the future.*

*We complain:*

*1. That nowhere in the world, with few exceptions, are black men accorded equal treatment with white men, although in the same situation and circumstances, but, on the contrary, are discriminated against and denied the common rights due to human beings for no other reason than their race and color.*

*We are not willingly accepted as guests in the public hotels and inns of the world for no other reason than our race and color.*

*2. In certain parts of the United States of America our race is denied the right of public trial accorded to other races when accused of crime, but are lynched and burned by mobs, and such brutal and inhuman treatment is even practiced upon our women.*

*3. That European nations have parcelled out among them and taken possession of nearly all of the continent of Africa, and the natives are compelled to surrender their lands to aliens and are treated in most instances like slaves.*

*4. In the southern portion of the United States of America, although citizens under the Federal Constitution, and in some States almost equal to the whites in population and are qualified land owners and taxpayers, we are, nevertheless, denied all voice in the making and administration of the laws and are taxed without representation by the State governments, and at the same time compelled to do military service in defense of the country.*

*5. On the public conveyances and common carriers in the southern portion of the United States we are jim-crowed and compelled to accept separate and inferior accommodations and made to pay the same fare charged for first-class accommodations, and our families are often humiliated and insulted by drunken white men who habitually pass through the jim-crow cars going to the smoking car.*

*6. The physicians of our race are denied the right to attend their patients while in the public hospitals of the cities and States where they reside in certain parts of the United States.*

*Our children are forced to attend inferior separate schools for shorter terms than white children, and the public school funds are unequally divided between the white and colored schools.*

*7. We are discriminated against and denied an equal chance to earn wages for the support of our families, and in many instances are refused admission into labor unions and nearly everywhere are paid smaller wages than white men.*

*8. In the Civil Service and departmental offices we are everywhere discriminated against and made to feel that to be a black man in Europe, America and the West Indies is equivalent to being an outcast and a leper among the races of men, no matter what the character attainments of the black men may be.*

*9. In the British and other West Indian islands and
colonies Negroes are secretly and cunningly
discriminated against and denied those fuller rights of
government to which white citizens are appointed,
nominated and elected.*

*10. That our people in those parts are forced to work for
lower wages than the average standard of white men and
are kept in conditions repugnant to good civilized tastes
and customs.*

*11. That the many acts of injustices against members of
our race before the courts of law in the respective islands
and colonies are of such nature as to create disgust and
disrespect for the white man's sense of justice.*

*12. Against all such inhuman, unchristian and
uncivilized treatment we here and now emphatically
protest, and invoke the condemnation of all mankind.*

*In order to encourage our race all over the world and to
stimulate it to overcome the handicaps and difficulties
surrounding it, and to push forward to a higher and
grander destiny, we demand and insist on the following
Declaration of Rights:*

*1. Be it known to all men that whereas all men are created
equal and entitled to the rights of life, liberty and the
pursuit of happiness, and because of this we, the duly
elected representatives of the Negro peoples of the world,
invoking the aid of the just and Almighty God, do declare
all men, women and children of our blood throughout the
world free denizens, and do claim them as free citizens of
Africa, the Motherland of all Negroes.*

*2. That we believe in the supreme authority of our race in
all things racial; that all things are created and given to
man as a common possession; that there should be an
equitable distribution and apportionment of all such
things, and in consideration of the fact that as a race we
are now deprived of those things that are morally and
legally ours, we believed it right that all such things*

*should be acquired and held by whatsoever means possible.*

*3. That we believe the Negro, like any other race, should be governed by the ethics of civilization, and therefore should not be deprived of any of those rights or privileges common to other human beings.*

*4. We declare that Negroes, wheresoever they form a community among themselves should be given the right to elect their own representatives to represent them in Legislatures, courts of law, or such institutions as may exercise control over that particular community.*

*5. We assert that the Negro is entitled to even-handed justice before all courts of law and equity in whatever country he may be found, and when this is denied him on account of his race or color such denial is an insult to the race as a whole and should be resented by the entire body of Negroes.*

*6. We declare it unfair and prejudicial to the rights of Negroes in communities where they exist in considerable numbers to be tried by a judge and jury composed entirely of an alien race, but in all such cases members of our race are entitled to representation on the jury.*

*7. We believe that any law or practice that tends to deprive any African of his land or the privileges of free citizenship within his country is unjust and immoral, and no native should respect any such law or practice.*

*8. We declare taxation without representation unjust and tyran[n]ous, and there should be no obligation on the part of the Negro to obey the levy of a tax by any law-making body from which he is excluded and denied representation on account of his race and color.*

*9. We believe that any law especially directed against the Negro to his detriment and singling him out because of his race or color is unfair and immoral, and should not be respected.*

*10. We believe all men entitled to common human respect and that our race should in no way tolerate any insults*

*that may be interpreted to mean disrespect to our race or
color.*

*11. We deprecate the use of the term "nigger" as applied
to Negroes, and demand that the word "Negro" be
written with a capital "N."*

*12. We believe that the Negro should adopt every means
to protect himself against barbarous practices inflicted
upon him because of color.*

*13. We believe in the freedom of Africa for the Negro
people of the world, and by the principle of Europe for the
Europeans and Asia for the Asiatics, we also demand
Africa for the Africans at home and abroad.*

*14. We believe in the inherent right of the Negro to
possess himself of Africa and that his possession of same
shall not be regarded as an infringement of any claim or
purchase made by any race or nation.*

*15. We strongly condemn the cupidity of those nations of
the world who, by open aggression or secret schemes,
have seized the territories and inexhaustible natural
wealth of Africa, and we place on record our most solemn
determination to reclaim the treasures and possession of
the vast continent of our forefathers.*

*16. We believe all men should live in peace one with the
other, but when races and nations provoke the ire of other
races and nations by attempting to infringe upon their
rights[,] war becomes inevitable, and the attempt in any
way to free one's self or protect one's rights or heritage
becomes justifiable.*

*17. Whereas the lynching, by burning, hanging or any
other means, of human beings is a barbarous practice and
a shame and disgrace to civilization, we therefore declare
any country guilty of such atrocities outside the pale of
civilization.*

*18. We protest against the atrocious crime of whipping,
flogging and overworking of the native tribes of Africa
and Negroes everywhere. These are methods that should*

*be abolished and all means should be taken to prevent a continuance of such brutal practices.*

*19. We protest against the atrocious practice of shaving the heads of Africans, especially of African women or individuals of Negro blood, when placed in prison as a punishment for crime by an alien race.*

*10. We protest against segregated districts, separate public conveyances, industrial discrimination, lynchings and limitations of political privileges of any Negro citizen in any part of the world on account of race, color or creed, and will exert our full influence and power against all such.*

*21. We protest against any punishment inflicted upon a Negro with severity, as against lighter punishment inflicted upon another of an alien race for like offense, as an act of prejudice and injustice, and should be resented by the entire race.*

*22. We protest against the system of education in any country where Negroes are denied the same privileges and advantages as other races.*

*23. We declare it inhuman and unfair to boycott Negroes from industries and labor in any part of the world.*

*24. We believe in the doctrine of the freedom of the press, and we therefore emphatically protest against the suppression of Negro newspapers and periodicals in various parts of the world, and call upon Negroes everywhere to employ all available means to prevent such suppression.*

*25. We further demand free speech universally for all men.*

*26. We hereby protest against the publication of scandalous and inflammatory articles by an alien press tending to create racial strife and the exhibition of picture films showing the Negro as a cannibal.*

*27. We believe in the self-determination of all peoples.*

*28. We declare for the freedom of religious worship.*

*29. With the help of Almighty God we declare ourselves
the sworn protectors of the honor and virtue of our
women and children, and pledge our lives for their
protection and defense everywhere and under all
circumstances from wrongs and outrages.*

*30. We demand the right of an unlimited and
unprejudiced education for ourselves and our posterity
forever[.]*

*31. We declare that the teaching in any school by alien
teachers to our boys and girls, that the alien race is
superior to the Negro race, is an insult to the Negro
people of the world.*

*32. Where Negroes form a part of the citizenry of any
country, and pass the civil service examination of such
country, we declare them entitled to the same
consideration as other citizens as to appointments in such
civil service.*

*33. We vigorously protest against the increasingly unfair
and unjust treatment accorded Negro travelers on land
and sea by the agents and employee of railroad and
steamship companies, and insist that for equal fare we
receive equal privileges with travelers of other races.*

*34. We declare it unjust for any country, State or nation
to enact laws tending to hinder and obstruct the free
immigration of Negroes on account of their race and
color.*

*35. That the right of the Negro to travel unmolested
throughout the world be not abridged by any person or
persons, and all Negroes are called upon to give aid to a
fellow Negro when thus molested.*

*36. We declare that all Negroes are entitled to the same
right to travel over the world as other men.*

*37. We hereby demand that the governments of the world
recognize our leader and his representatives chosen by the
race to look after the welfare of our people under such
governments.*

38. *We demand complete control of our social institutions without interference by any alien race or races.*

39. *That the colors, Red, Black and Green, be the colors of the Negro race.*

40. *Resolved, That the anthem "Ethiopia, Thou Land of Our Fathers etc.," shall be the anthem of the Negro race. . . .*

41. *We believe that any limited liberty which deprives one of the complete rights and prerogatives of full citizenship is but a modified form of slavery.*

42. *We declare it an injustice to our people and a serious Impediment to the health of the race to deny to competent licensed Negro physicians the right to practice in the public hospitals of the communities in which they reside, for no other reason than their race and color.*

43. *We call upon the various government[s] of the world to accept and acknowledge Negro representatives who shall be sent to the said governments to represent the general welfare of the Negro peoples of the world.*

44. *We deplore and protest against the practice of confining juvenile prisoners in prisons with adults, and we recommend that such youthful prisoners be taught gainful trades under human[e] supervision.*

45. *Be it further resolved, That we as a race of people declare the League of Nations null and void as far as the Negro is concerned, in that it seeks to deprive Negroes of their liberty.*

46. *We demand of all men to do unto us as we would do unto them, in the name of justice; and we cheerfully accord to all men all the rights we claim herein for ourselves.*

47. *We declare that no Negro shall engage himself in battle for an alien race without first obtaining the consent of the leader of the Negro people of the world, except in a matter of national self-defense.*

48. *We protest against the practice of drafting Negroes and sending them to war with alien forces without proper*

*training, and demand in all cases that Negro soldiers be given the same training as the aliens.*

*49. We demand that instructions given Negro children in schools include the subject of "Negro History," to their benefit.*

*50. We demand a free and unfettered commercial intercourse with all the Negro people of the world.*

*51. We declare for the absolute freedom of the seas for all peoples.*

*52. We demand that our duly accredited representatives be given proper recognition in all leagues, conferences, conventions or courts of international arbitration wherever human rights are discussed.*

*53. We proclaim the 31st day of August of each year to be an international holiday to be observed by all Negroes.*

*54. We want all men to know that we shall maintain and contend for the freedom and equality of every man, woman and child of our race, with our lives, our fortunes and our sacred honor.*

*These rights we believe to be justly ours and proper for the protection of the Negro race at large, and because of this belief we, on behalf of the four hundred million Negroes of the world, do pledge herein the sacred blood of the race in defense, and we hereby subscribe our names as a guarantee of the truthfulness and faithfulness hereof, in the presence of Almighty God, on this 13th day of August, in the year of our Lord one thousand nine hundred and twenty.*

# *FOOTNOTES*

1.www.bjs.gov/content/pub/pdf/Pi94.pdf

2.HTTP://WWW.NAACP.ORG/PAGES/CRIMINAL-JUSTICE-FACT-SHEET

3.WWW.MASSHIST.ORG/DIGITALADAMS/ARCHIVE/DOC?ID=L1
7800512JASECOND

4.THE PRINCE BY NICOLO MACHIAVELLI CHAPTER XVII

5.THE ART OF WAR BY TSUN TZU JEFF MCNIELL CLASSICS, LLC,
2012

6.BEING LOGICAL: A GUIDE TO GOOD THINKING D.Q.
MCINERNY

7.https://www.ssa.gov/policy/docs/ssb/v64n4/v64n4p1.html

# References

1. *Black Access: A Bibliography of Afro-American Bibliographies*. 1984.
African American Research Center 016.9730496. N468BL. Helps "locate
information on virtually every aspect of Afro-American life, culture,
and history." Lists library catalogs, guides and separately published
bibliographies.

2. *Eight Negro bibliographies*. 1970. Main Stacks 016.301451 W67E.
Includes: The freedom rides.--The Southern students' protest
movement.--The University of Mississippi and James H. Meredith.--The
Black Muslims in the United States.--Martin Luther King, Jr., 1929-1968.-
-The awesome thunder of Booker T. Washington.--The lynching records
at Tuskegee Institute; with lynching in America.--The perilous road of
Marcus M. Garvey: A Bibliography, and some correspondence with
Booker T. Washington, Emmett J. Scott, and Robert Russa Moton.

3. *Harvard Guide to African-American History*. 2001. African American
Research Center 973.0496073 H261.  Includes more than 15,000 entries.
The first part of the *Guide* contains 12 essays on historical research aids,
from traditional archival and reference materials to the Internet. The
second and largest part presents comprehensive and chronological
bibliographies. The third part contains listings of resources on the
special subjects of women.

4. *In Black and White*. 3rd ed. 1980. 2 vols. + suppl. African American
Research Center 016.920073.SP71980.  A guide to magazine articles,
newspaper articles, and books concerning the careers and contributions
to society of more than 15,000 black individuals and groups. Includes
index to occupations.

Dr. Riyaad Giovanni

5. *Who's Who Among African Americans*. 9th ed. 1996- . African American Research Center 920.073.W62171.  Reference provides biographical and career details on more than 20,000 notable African American individuals, including leaders from sports, the arts, business, religion and more. An obituary section contains fully updated entries for listees who have died since the previous edition.

6. *Encyclopedia of the African Diaspora: Origins, Experiences, and Culture.* 3 vols.  2008.  African American Research Center 305.896003 En199.  More than 500 entries covering the people, places, and events of the African diaspora, spanning five continents and five centuries.  Organized in A–Z sections covering global topics, country of origin, and destination country.

7. *Afro-American Literature and Culture Since World War II: A Guide to Information Sources.* 1979.  Main Stacks 016.813.P32A.  An annotated post-World War II through 1970 bibliography.  Subjects include the civil rights movement, folklore, prison writing, riots, religion, women, and psychology, among others.  An Author section lists 56 authors including  Malcolm X, Martin Luther King Jr., Nikki Giovanni, W.E.B. Dubois, Ralph Ellison, Richard Wright, and Langston Hughes, among others.

8. *Afro-American Poetry and Drama, 1760-1975: A Guide to Information Sources.* 1979.  Main Reference 016.81.AF85.  Consists of two parts: Afro-American poetry, 1760-1975 and Afro-American drama,  1850-1975. Both sections are divided into General Studies containing works of reference, history and criticism and Individual Authors listing an author's books of poetry as well as biographical and critical studies. *Bibliographical Guide to African-American Women Writers.* 1993.  African American Research Center 016.8108.J761B.  Documents the literary achievements of 900 African American women from 1746 to the present in thousands of primary and secondary sources.  Writers are arranged in alphabetically and include a list of primary sources entered

alphabetically by title, followed by secondary sources entered by
author.

9. *Black Literature Criticism.* 3 vols. 1992. African American Research
Center 809.8896.B5616. Contains critical excerpts on some 125
internationally prominent black authors of the 18th, 19th, and 20th
centuries. Each author entry includes an introduction that covers
biographical details, the major literary interests of the author,
descriptions and summaries of the author's best known works, and
critical commentary about the author's achievement, status, and
importance; a chronological list of principal works; and multiple
excerpts of criticism, including book reviews, academic studies of
individual works, and comparative studies, arranged chronologically to
give a sense of how critical reception evolved over time.

10. *Black Literature Criticism: Classic and Emerging Authors since 1950.* 2nd
ed. 3 vols. 2008. African American Research Center 809.889
B561. Covers 80 authors, the majority of whom are African American,
but representative African and Caribbean authors are also included.
Each entry presents a historical survey of critical response to the
author's works.

11. *Contemporary African American Novelists: A Bio-bibliographical Critical
Sourcebook.* 1999. African American Research Center 813.09 C7674. This
reference book is a guide to the lives, works, and achievements of 79
contemporary African American novelists. Of the 79 novelists profiled,
41 are women. Each entry has a biographical sketch of the author, a
critical assessment of the author's major works and themes, a sample of
critical responses the author's novels have elicited, and a selected
bibliography listing the author's publications as well as useful
secondary material.

12. *Encyclopedia of African American Business History. 1999. African American Research Center 338.6422 En19.* Provides an overview of black business activities, and underscores the existence of a historic tradition of black American business participation. Entries range from biographies of black business people to overview surveys of business activities from the 1600s to the 1990s, including slave and free black business activities and the Black Wallstreet to coverage of black women's business activities, and discussions of such African American specific industries as catering, funeral enterprises, insurance, and hair care and cosmetic products. Also, there are entries on blacks in the automotive parts industry, black investment banks, black companies listed on the stock market, blacks and corporate America, civil rights and black business, and black athletes and business activities. *Encyclopedia of African-American Civil Rights: From Emancipation to the Present.* 1992. African American Research Center 305.896073.EN19. Contains over 800 short articles. Covers a wide array of events, legislation, court decisions, cultural achievements, speeches, organizations, and personalities that have contributed to the cause of African American civil rights. Also includes a detailed chronology from 1861 to 1990.

13. *Encyclopedia of African American Education. 2010.* 2 vols. African American Research Center 371.82996.En192. The encyclopedia follows the struggle of African Americans to achieve equality in education--beginning among an enslaved population and evolving into the present--as the efforts of many remarkable individuals furthered this cause through court decisions and legislation. Entries provide an overview of educational institutions at every level, from preschool through graduate and professional training, with special attention to historically and predominantly Black colleges and universities. A unique appendix, "The Complete Bibliography of the *Journal of Negro Education,* 1932-2008," includes listings of the tables of contents and reprinted articles on segregation, desegregation, and equality.

*14. Encyclopedia of African-American Politics.* 2003. African American
Research Center 973.0496073 Sm644e. Containing more than 400
entries, this volume examines the role of African Americans in the
political process from the American Revolution to the present. It
focuses on basic political ideas, court cases, laws, concepts, ideologies,
institutions, and political processes.

*15. Encyclopedia of African American Society.* 2005. 2 vols. African
American Research Center 305.896072 En192. The first comprehensive
reference set in this field to give voice to the turbulent historical trends--
slavery, segregation, "separate but equal" --that are often ignored in
favor of mere facts. Also contains hundreds of articles on notable
African Americans (Martin Luther King, Jr., Jackie Robinson, Miles
Davis), groundbreaking events (Emancipation Proclamation, Los
Angeles Riots), sports and culture (Rap Music, Jazz), and significant
heritage sites (Apollo Theater).

*16. Encyclopedia ff American Race Riots.* 2007. 2 vols. African American
Research Center 305.80097303 En192. Topics include: particular riots
and violent racial incidents; the African American community's
preparedness and responses to this form of mass violence; federal
responses to rioting; the underlying causes of rioting; reactions of
prominent figures. Besides almost 300 cross-referenced entries, most of
which conclude with lists of additional readings, the encyclopedia also
offers a timeline of racial violence in the United States, an extensive
bibliography, and a selection of primary documents.
*Freedom Facts And Firsts: 400 Years Of The African American Civil Rights
Experience.* 2009. African American Research Center 323.1196073
Sm613f. Spanning nearly 400 years from the early abolitionists to the
present, this guide book profiles more than 400 people, places, and
events that have shaped the history of the black struggle for freedom.
Coverage includes information on such mainstays as Martin Luther
King, Jr., Malcolm X, and Rosa Parks, and lesser known figures such as
the Housewives' League of Detroit.

17. *The Jim Crow Encyclopedia*. 2008. 2 vols. African American Research Center 305.896073 J564. Jim Crow refers to a set of laws in many states, predominantly in the South, after the end of Reconstruction in 1877 that severely restricted the rights and privileges of African Americans. Includes 275 essay entries on such areas as law, media, business, politics, employment, religion, education, people, events, culture, the arts, protest, the military, class, housing, sports, and violence as well as through accompanying key primary documents excerpted as side bars.

## ABOUT THE AUTHOR

I am a man! Do Not tread on me! I am dedicated to God, Family, Community & Economic Independence For Black People. **I am unapologetically Black!**